TOUCHSTONE

MICHAEL McCARTHY
JEANNE McCARTEN
HELEN SANDIFORD

3A

WITH

LISA HUTCHINS
JENNIFER WILKIN

WORKBOOK

CAMBRIDGE
UNIVERSITY PRESS

CAMBRIDGE UNIVERSITY PRESS
Cambridge, New York, Melbourne, Madrid, Cape Town,
Singapore, São Paulo, Delhi, Mexico City

Cambridge University Press
32 Avenue of the Americas, New York, NY 10013-2473, USA

www.cambridge.org
Information on this title: www.cambridge.org/9780521601429

First published 2006
5th printing 2012

Printed in Lima, Peru, by Empresa Editora El Comercio S.A.

A catalog record for this publication is available from the British Library.

ISBN   978-0-521-66599-5   pack consisting of student's book and self-study audio cd/cd-rom (Windows®, Mac®)
ISBN   978-0-521-60139-9   pack consisting of student's book/Korea and self-study audio cd/cd-rom (Windows®, Mac®)
ISBN   978-0-521-60140-5   pack consisting of student's book A and self-study audio cd/cd-rom (Windows®, Mac®)
ISBN   978-0-521-60141-2   pack consisting of student's book B and self-study audio cd/cd-rom (Windows®, Mac®)
ISBN   978-0-521-66598-8   workbook
ISBN   978-0-521-60142-9   workbook A
ISBN   978-0-521-60143-6   workbook B
ISBN   978-0-521-66597-1   teacher's edition
ISBN   978-0-521-66594-0   cds (audio)
ISBN   978-0-521-66595-7   cassettes

Art direction, book design, photo research, and layout services: Adventure House, NYC

Contents

Unit 1 The way we are

People in a hurry

1 Opposites

Grammar
and
vocabulary

Look at the pictures. Correct the sentences to match the pictures.

1. Craig is a careful driver.

   Craig is a reckless driver.

2. Lucia always arrives early.

3. Carlos is waiting impatiently.

4. Emily walks slowly.

5. Laila is talking loudly.

6. Tom seems polite.

7. Tamara plays tennis badly.

8. Joe and Kay are dressed inappropriately.

2 My new job!

Circle the correct words to complete Cleo's e-mail.

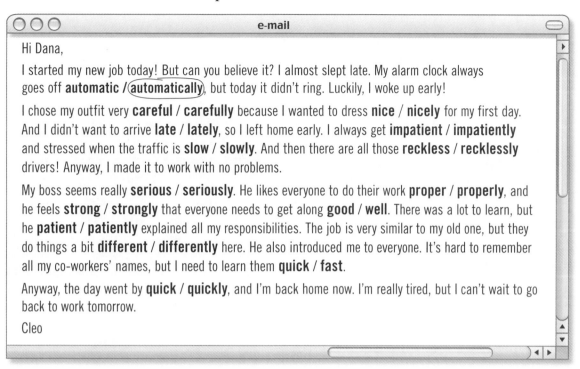

○○○   e-mail

Hi Dana,

I started my new job today! But can you believe it? I almost slept late. My alarm clock always goes off **automatic /** (**automatically**), but today it didn't ring. Luckily, I woke up early!

I chose my outfit very **careful / carefully** because I wanted to dress **nice / nicely** for my first day. And I didn't want to arrive **late / lately**, so I left home early. I always get **impatient / impatiently** and stressed when the traffic is **slow / slowly**. And then there are all those **reckless / recklessly** drivers! Anyway, I made it to work with no problems.

My boss seems really **serious / seriously**. He likes everyone to do their work **proper / properly**, and he feels **strong / strongly** that everyone needs to get along **good / well**. There was a lot to learn, but he **patient / patiently** explained all my responsibilities. The job is very similar to my old one, but they do things a bit **different / differently** here. He also introduced me to everyone. It's hard to remember all my co-workers' names, but I need to learn them **quick / fast**.

Anyway, the day went by **quick / quickly**, and I'm back home now. I'm really tired, but I can't wait to go back to work tomorrow.

Cleo

3 Are you fast?

A Complete the answers with an adjective or adverb. Sometimes more than one answer is possible.

1. *A* Are you a fast reader?
   B No, actually, I read very _____slowly_____ .
2. *A* Do you think you're lazy?
   B No, actually, I'm a _____ worker.
3. *A* Do you have difficulty remembering names?
   B I don't think so. I remember names very _____ .
4. *A* Do you eat your meals quickly?
   B Yes, I'm a _____ eater.
5. *A* Are you a good singer?
   B Well, no. People say I sing _____ .
6. *A* Are you good at sports?
   B Yes, I play most sports _____ .

B Write true answers to the questions in part A.

1. _Yes, I am. I read everything very quickly._ _____
2. _____
3. _____
4. _____
5. _____
6. _____

3

Personality and character

1 What are they like?

A There are eight personality words in the puzzle. Find the other seven.
Look in these directions (→↓).

P	R	A	C	T	I	C	A	L	O	D
D	P	L	O	A	T	B	F	K	S	I
L	O	R	E	L	I	A	B	L	E	S
T	G	T	P	E	B	M	D	W	L	O
A	F	V	J	N	P	C	I	H	F	R
Q	B	I	E	T	S	H	V	N	I	G
H	G	E	N	E	R	O	U	S	S	A
R	K	E	L	D	G	O	K	D	H	N
U	O	U	T	G	O	I	N	G	T	I
O	Y	C	R	L	S	Q	E	Y	I	Z
E	A	S	Y	G	O	I	N	G	Q	E
X	B	A	I	H	P	N	T	A	Z	D

B Complete the sentences with the words from part A.

1. My aunt likes to paint. She has creative ideas and is incredibly __talented__ .
2. Ellie is totally _____ . She can never find her car keys and is always losing her cell phone.
3. My friend Steve is extremely down-to-earth and _____ . He gives useful advice.
4. Bill is really _____ . He isn't shy at all.
5. My dad bought me a laptop computer for college. He's very kind and _____ like that.
6. Max is usually good about completing his work. He's fairly _____ .
7. Alice is pretty laid-back and _____ . She never gets upset about anything.
8. My little sister never shares anything. She's so _____ !

2 About you 1

Complete each question with the opposite of the adjective given.
Then write true answers.

1. Are you honest or __dishonest__ ? __I'm honest. I always tell the truth.__
2. Is your doctor friendly or _____ ? _____
3. Is your best friend reliable or _____ ? _____
4. Are you organized or _____ ? _____
5. Are you patient or _____ ? _____
6. Are your neighbors considerate or _____ ? _____

3 All or nothing

What's the best next sentence? Circle *a* or *b*.

1. Brian's not talented at all.
   a. He sings, dances, and acts.
   (b.) He can't sing, dance, or act!

2. Jennifer's extremely generous.
   a. She gives a lot of money to charity.
   b. She gives a little money to charity.

3. My sister is incredibly smart.
   a. She's the best student in her class.
   b. She does fairly well in school.

4. Amir is so funny.
   a. His jokes don't make me laugh at all.
   b. His jokes always make me laugh.

5. Samantha is fairly outgoing.
   a. She never goes to parties.
   b. She sometimes goes to parties.

6. My math teacher is really helpful.
   a. She gives great explanations.
   b. She sometimes gives bad explanations.

7. Adam is pretty laid-back.
   a. He gets upset about everything.
   b. He doesn't get upset about most things.

8. Jack is completely inconsiderate.
   a. He never helps his family around the house.
   b. He sometimes helps his family around the house.

4 About you 2

Use the expressions in the box to write true sentences about someone you know. Then add a second sentence about yourself.

fairly easygoing	not impatient at all	really practical
incredibly friendly	✓ pretty reliable	very honest

1. My older brother's pretty reliable. I think I'm pretty unreliable.
2. _____
3. _____
4. _____
5. _____
6. _____

He's always working.

1 They're always . . .

Conversation strategies The people in this office don't work very hard. Look at the picture, and write what each person is always doing.

1. Jedd _is always leaving work early_ . 4. Kayo _____ .

2. Reba _____ . 5. Yasmin _____ .

3. John _____ . 6. Chad _____ .

2 Individual habits

Conversation strategies Write a response to each statement with *always* and a continuous verb. Use the expressions in the box.

| buy things ✓cancel plans help people lose stuff tell jokes |

1. Beth is so unreliable.   I know. _She's always canceling plans!_ _____

2. Matt is incredibly disorganized.   That's for sure. _____

3. Elizabeth is very funny.   That's true. _____

4. Theresa isn't practical with money.   You're right. _____

5. Kenny is generous with his time.   Yeah, he is. _____

6

3 Complaints, complaints

Complete each conversation with *always* and a continuous verb. Then add *at least* to the response when appropriate.

1. **Sam** My sister hardly ever talks to my friends when they come over. She **'s always doing** (do) something else. I mean, she says "Hi," but that's all.

    Fatema Well, _____ she isn't rude to them.

2. **Jody** Last year, my roommate in college _____ (borrow) my books and stuff without asking.

    Pam That's too bad – _____ it sounds like she was really inconsiderate.

3. **Sandy** My last boss was really nice but completely disorganized. She _____ (cancel) meetings at the last minute.

    Natsuko Yeah, _____ it's hard to work for somebody like that.

4. **Daniel** My brother _____ (listen) to his MP3 player. He's always got his headphones on.

    Sarah Well, _____ his music isn't loud.

5. **Alejandro** I never see my kids these days. They _____ (go) to their friends' houses to play basketball or baseball or something.

    Diana Well, you know, _____ they're interested in sports. A lot of kids just play computer games all the time.

4 About you

Complete each sentence with true information. Use *always* and a continuous verb.

1. When I was little, **I was always eating candy** .
2. My friends and I _____ .
3. I have some bad habits. I _____ .
4. My best friend _____ .
5. My parents _____ .
6. My favorite teacher in high school _____ .
7. My neighbor _____ .

1 Star qualities

Reading | **A** Read the article. Circle the two adjectives that describe actor Aishwarya Rai in each column.

(famous)	accomplished	inconsiderate	generous
arrogant	influential	down-to-earth	unfriendly
talented	selfish	beautiful	nice

Aishwarya Rai
THE QUEEN OF BOLLYWOOD

Aishwarya Rai is the Queen of Bollywood, India's version of Hollywood and the film capital of the world. With over 18,000 Web sites devoted to her, she is India's, and possibly the world's, best-known actor. Yet, perhaps surprisingly, Rai still lives at home with her parents.

Aishwarya Rai was born in Mangalore, India, on November 1, 1973. She was raised in a traditional, middle-class family. When she was four, her family moved to Mumbai (Bombay), where she still lives today.

Rai started modeling for fun when she was in college studying architecture. She also received many offers to act.

However, her first priority was school, so she said no to all movie offers. Then in 1994, at the age of 21, Rai won the title of Miss World. Soon after that, she accepted her first movie role.

Now an accomplished actor, Rai won Filmfare's Award for Best Actress for her role in *Hum Dil De Chuke Sanam* in

2000. She also starred in Bollywood's most successful international blockbuster, *Devdas*. Rai acts in five different languages: Hindi, Kannada, Tamil, Urdu, and English.

In 2004, Rai was in *Time* magazine's list of the 100 most influential people in the world, and it's easy to see why. She is the first Bollywood star to be a juror at the Cannes Film Festival in France, to appear in *Rolling Stone* magazine, and to be on *The Oprah Winfrey Show*. Rai is also the first Indian woman to have a statue in London's wax museum, Madame Tussaud's.

Aishwarya Rai is one of the most beautiful women in the world, but when Oprah Winfrey asked her about her beauty, she simply said, "Beauty is as beauty does," meaning that what you do is more important than how you look. This is perhaps why Rai created a charitable organization called the Aishwarya Rai Foundation, which helps women, children, the elderly, and animals. Her philosophy is very simple: "It's nice to be important, but it's important to be nice."

B Read Rai's biography again. Then correct these false sentences.

1. Aishwarya Rai lives ~~by herself~~ *with her parents* in Mumbai.

2. Rai was born in Mumbai.

3. Rai started modeling in high school.

4. Rai studied acting in college.

5. Rai won the title of Miss World when she was 19.

6. Rai makes movies in four languages.

7. Rai has a statue in Cannes, France.

8. Rai feels that it's important to be beautiful.

2 She's admirable.

Writing **A** Use the words and expressions in the box to complete the profile of Midori Goto.

accomplished	called	started
at the age of	can be	✓was born and raised

Midori Goto

Midori Goto is an incredibly talented violinist. She ___was born and raised___ in Osaka, Japan. She _____ studying the violin with her mother, and _____ seven, she gave her first public performance in Osaka.

Studying music _____ very demanding, as well as rewarding. When she was only 10, Midori moved to New York City to study music at the Juilliard School. She also attended the Professional Children's School for her academic studies. By the time Midori turned 11, she was already an _____ artist and had performed with the New York Philharmonic.

Midori is also very generous. In 1992, she created an organization _____ Midori & Friends that provides free music education for children in city schools.

B Write a short profile about someone you admire.

Unit 1 Progress chart

Mark the boxes below to rate your progress. ☑ = I know how to . . . [?] = I need to review how to . . .	To review, go back to these pages in the Student's Book.
Grammar ☐ use manner adverbs and adjectives correctly	2 and 3
☐ use regular and irregular adverbs	3
☐ use adverbs to make adjectives and adverbs stronger	5
☐ add prefixes to adjectives to make opposites	5
Vocabulary ☐ name at least 12 adverbs	2, 3, 4, and 5
☐ name at least 15 personality adjectives	4 and 5
Conversation strategies ☐ use *always* and a continuous verb to describe individual habits	6
☐ use *at least* to point out the positive side of a situation	7
Writing ☐ write a short profile about someone	9

Unit 2 Experiences

Hopes and dreams

1 Have you or haven't you?

Grammar **A** Read the "to do" list. What things have you done? What things haven't you done? Write true sentences using the present perfect.

Things I want to do
1. *drive a sports car*
2. *go skiing*
3. *learn a second language*
4. *see the Taj Mahal*
5. *study photography*
6. *travel to Europe*
7. *try windsurfing*
8. *win an award*

1. _I haven't driven a sports car._
2. _____
3. _____
4. _____
5. _____
6. _____
7. _____
8. _____

B Complete the sentences using the present perfect and the expressions in the "to do" list in part A. Use the negative form where necessary.

1. Len _has driven a sports car_ once or twice. He loves to drive.
2. My sister and I _____ many times. We love the snow.
3. My brothers _____ . One speaks Mandarin and one speaks Cantonese.
4. We _____ , but I really want to go to India one day.
5. My teacher _____ . She takes beautiful travel photos.
6. Sol and Rhea _____ before, but they hope to go next year.
7. Gary _____ . He's afraid of the water.
8. Megan _____ for being the school's fastest swimmer.

10

2 *I've tried . . .*

Grammar **Write sentences with the present perfect.**

1. My teacher (go / many times) to the United States.
   <u>My teacher's been to the United States many times.</u>
   or <u>My teacher's gone to the United States many times.</u>

2. My boss (ski / several times) in the Swiss Alps.
   _____

3. I (always / want) to go on a roller coaster.
   _____

4. My neighbor (never / go / before) to Canada.
   _____

5. My parents (see / five times) the movie *Dr. Zhivago*.
   _____

6. My brothers (try / once or twice) Vietnamese food.
   _____

3 *About you*

Grammar **Answer the questions with true information. Add a frequency expression where necessary.**

1. What's something exciting you've done?
   <u>I've gone skydiving once.</u>

2. What's something scary you've done?
   _____

3. What's something boring you've done in the last month?
   _____

4. How many times have you been late to class recently?
   _____

5. What country have you always wanted to visit?
   _____

6. What kind of food have you never tried before?
   _____

7. What movie have you seen several times?
   _____

1 Have you ever . . . ?

Grammar   **Complete the conversations with the simple past or present perfect.**

1. *A* ___Have___ you ever ___gone___ (go) cliff diving?
   B No, I _____ . It sounds too scary!
      _____ you _____ (do) it?
   A Yeah, I _____ (go) last weekend.
   B Wow! You're brave. How _____ (be) it?
   A It was incredible! I _____ (love) it.

2. *A* I _____ never _____ (travel) alone.
      How about you?
   B No, but I _____ always _____ (want) to. I'm
      sure it's exciting.
   A I think so, too. Do you know my friend Jill?
      She _____ (take) a hiking trip alone last year.
   B I know. I _____ (speak) to her about it last week.

3. *A* _____ you ever _____ (try) horseback
      riding?
   B Yeah. I actually _____ (do) it once several
      years ago.
   A Really? _____ you _____ (like) it?
   B No, not really. It _____ (be) very scary.
   A Oh, too bad. I go all the time. I _____ (get)
      really good.

4. *A* _____ you _____ (do) anything special
      last weekend?
   B Yes. My husband and I _____ (take) a ride in a
      hot-air balloon! _____ you ever _____ (be)
      in one before?
   A No, I _____ . _____ you _____ (enjoy) it?
   B Yeah, we _____ (love) every minute! It was
      amazing!

2 Yes or no?

Grammar
and
vocabulary

Complete the questions with the simple past or present perfect form of the
verbs in the box. Then answer the questions with true information.

break	eat	✓go	have	lose	ride	visit	win

1. __Did__ you __go__ to the zoo yesterday? _No, I didn't go to the zoo yesterday._
2. _____ you ever _____ your leg? _____
3. _____ you ever _____ a spelling contest? _____
4. _____ you _____ a bike to school yesterday? _____
5. _____ you _____ your grandparents last summer? _____
6. _____ you ever _____ a bad cold? _____
7. _____ you _____ a big breakfast this morning? _____
8. _____ you ever _____ your wallet? _____

3 About you

Grammar

Use the cues to write questions in the simple past or present perfect.
Then write true answers.

1. (try any new foods / on your last vacation)
    Did you try any new foods on your last vacation?
    Yes, I did. I tried oysters. They're delicious.

2. (ever / hike in the mountains)
    _____
    _____

3. (see a lot of movies / last summer)
    _____
    _____

4. (ever / walk across a tightrope)
    _____
    _____

5. (ever / find someone's cell phone)
    _____
    _____

6. (ever / forget a friend's birthday)
    _____
    _____

1 Tell me more!

Complete the conversations with the responses in the box.

> Cool. Do you have a favorite place?
> I've heard her tests are hard. How did you do?
> Oh, that sounds hard. Did you finish?
>
> That sounds great. How do you get there?
> That's too bad. Did you study?
> ✓ Yeah, I am. Do you want to come?

1. *Jake* Hey, Alex! Are you going surfing this weekend?

   Alex <u>Yeah, I am. Do you want to come?</u>

   Jake Well, I'm working this weekend. And, actually, I've never surfed before.

   Alex Really? I started surfing three years ago, and now I can't stop.

   Jake _____

   Alex Yeah, I like to go to Cove Beach. Have you heard of it?

   Jake Yeah, I have, but I've never been there.

   Alex You should come sometime. I can teach you the basics.

   Jake _____

   Alex I usually drive. You can ride your bike there, but it's a bit far.

   Jake All right. Tell me the next time you're planning to go.

2. *Ki Won* Hi, Erin. You look upset. What's wrong?

   Erin I just took Mrs. Chen's English test.

   Ki Won _____

   Erin I don't think I did too well.

   Ki Won _____

   Erin Yeah, I studied really hard.

   Ki Won Was it an essay or a multiple-choice test?

   Erin Well, it was both. There were 30 multiple-choice questions *and* an essay question!

   Ki Won _____

   Erin Yeah, I finished it, but I didn't have time to check my answers.

   Ki Won Well, maybe you did better than you think!

2 Did you?

Complete each conversation with a response question to show interest.

1. *A* I went on a roller coaster last weekend.
   B _Did you?_ That sounds like fun.

2. *A* I love going to the movies!
   B _____ Let's go sometime!

3. *A* I won first prize in the art contest!
   B _____ That's wonderful!

4. *A* I'm really afraid of both snakes and spiders.
   B _____ I am too.

5. *A* I ride my motorcycle on the weekends.
   B _____ I've never ridden a motorcycle.

6. *A* I've broken my arm twice.
   B _____ That's too bad.

7. *A* I'm 18 years old today!
   B _____ Happy birthday!

8. *A* I've seen the new Tom Cruise movie 20 times.
   B _____ Is he your favorite actor?

3 Extreme sports

Respond to these statements with a response question. Then add a follow-up question to ask for more information.

1. In the summer, I love to go hang gliding. Do you? Is it scary? _____

2. I've gone scuba diving several times. _____

3. Last spring, I went deep-sea fishing. _____

4. I'm a pretty good windsurfer. _____

5. I absolutely love sailing. _____

6. I started surfing last year. _____

1 *Finally here!*

Reading **A** Read Gisele's travel blog about her trip to Chile. Where has she always wanted to go?

○○○   **Gisele's Blog**

Gisele   **Finally here!**

We arrived yesterday morning in Pucón, in Chile's Lake District. We're exhausted from traveling, but Pucón seems like a fun place, and we'll stay here for the next few days. Today we rented a canoe and went swimming in the lake. There's also an active volcano nearby – you can see it from the lake. It's really cool to see smoke coming out of the top!

Our hotel is great. It's right in the middle of town, and it has a café where a lot of people come to hang out. There are a lot of travelers here because it's cheap and the food is good. We met some people from Canada last night. They've been to the national park where we plan to go next, so we got lots of useful information from them.

We haven't decided where to stay in Torres del Paine National Park. Has anyone ever been there? Is it better to camp or stay in the *refugios*?

Posted January 25, at 9:57 a.m.

TravelJoe   **Re: Finally here!**

The *refugios* are nice places to stay. They're like lodges – some even have cafeterias – but I think camping is a good option this time of year. The *refugios* will be too crowded. I was at Torres del Paine in February two years ago, and the weather was perfect for camping. Good luck!

Posted January 26, at 10:24 p.m.

Gisele   **Last day in Pucón**

Today we went horseback riding to see some waterfalls. I was worried about falling off the horse, but it was OK. We saw some scenery that you can't see on foot, and it was spectacular.

Tomorrow we leave for Torres del Paine. I'm so excited – I've always wanted to go to Patagonia! Thanks for the info, TravelJoe. We brought our tents along, just in case.

Posted January 28, at 8:19 p.m.

Gisele   **Wow!**

We just spent a week in Torres del Paine. We did the "W," which is a five-day hike that zigzags through the park. We stopped to camp each night along the way. Fortunately, it didn't rain. It was amazing! We saw pink flamingos and a guanaco, which is an animal that looks like a furry horse with a llama's head. The mountains were awesome. I didn't want to leave. Tonight we stay in Santiago, and then it's to the airport and home.

Posted February 5, at 4:45 p.m.

B Read the blog again. Then answer the questions.

1. When did Gisele arrive in Pucón? <u>She arrived in Pucón on January 24.</u>

2. Why is her hotel popular with travelers? _____

3. What did the Canadians tell her about? _____

4. Why does TravelJoe think she should camp in Torres del Paine? _____

    _____

5. How long does it take to do the "W" hike? _____

6. Where did Gisele sleep in Torres del Paine? _____

2 *Fortunately, . . .*

Writing **A** Read Ian's blog entry about his trip to Belize. Complete the sentences with
fortunately, unfortunately, or *amazingly.*

○○○   Ian's Blog

Ian   We were very tired when we got off the plane in Belize City, but __fortunately__ , our host was there to meet us. _____ , the airline lost my luggage, so I left the airport without it. We got on a bus and headed for Maya Mountain Lodge. _____ , when we got to the lodge, my luggage was already there! The next morning, we set out on our first trip. The mountain road was narrow and curvy. _____ , our driver drove carefully. Our first stop was at a big waterfall. _____ , it was raining when we got there, so we just took pictures from the bus. Our next stop was at a river called Rio on Pools. It was hot, so everyone went swimming. _____ , I didn't have my bathing suit with me, so I couldn't go. The views were so beautiful that I took a lot of pictures. I'm not usually a good photographer, but _____ , my pictures were great.

B Write a blog entry about one of the following experiences. Use adverbs
like *fortunately* and *amazingly* to show your feelings about what happened.

- Competing in a contest
- Having a fun picnic
- Taking an exciting trip
- Trying a new activity

○○○   Blog

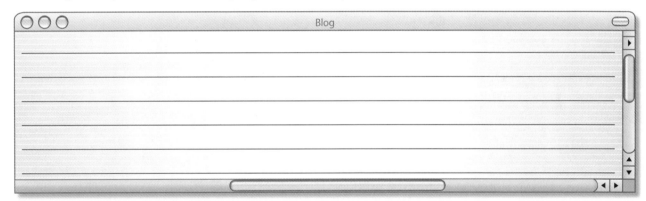

Unit 2 Progress chart

Mark the boxes below to rate your progress. ☑ = I know how to . . . ? = I need to review how to . . .	To review, go back to these pages in the Student's Book.
Grammar	
☐ use the present perfect with regular and irregular verbs	12 and 13
☐ use the present perfect to say what I have and haven't done	13, 14, and 15
☐ ask and answer questions beginning with *Have you ever . . . ?*	14 and 15
☐ use the simple past to answer questions in the present perfect	14 and 15
Vocabulary	
☐ name at least 12 irregular past participles	13, 14, and 15
Conversation strategies	
☐ keep a conversation going by showing interest	16
☐ use *Do you?, Did you?, Are you?,* or *Have you?* to show interest	17
Writing	
☐ use adverbs to show my feelings about something	19

Unit 3 Wonders of the world

Human wonders

1 That's expensive!

Grammar and vocabulary

Complete the questions with superlatives. Then match the questions with the correct pictures and information below.

1. What's _the most expensive_ (expensive) musical instrument ever sold? _h_
2. Which country has _____ (long) school year? ____
3. What sport has _____ (fans) in the world? ____
4. Who's _____ (young) number-one classical artist? ____
5. Where's _____ (small) house in the world? ____
6. What's _____ (famous) statue in the United States? ____
7. What's one of _____ (tall) hotels in the world? ____
8. What's _____ (fast) car in the world? ____

a) The Burj al-Arab Hotel in Dubai is 321 meters (1,060 feet) tall.

b) Almost 4 million people visit the Statue of Liberty each year.

c) Millions of fans around the world watch soccer.

d) The Thrust SSC can go up to 1,227 kilometers (763 miles) per hour.

e) Welsh soprano Charlotte Church was only 12 years old when her album, *Voice of an Angel*, sold over two million copies in the UK.

f) Chinese children go to school 251 days a year.

g) The Quay House in Conwy, Wales, is 3.09 meters high by 1.8 meters wide (10 feet high by 5.9 feet wide).

h) "The Lady Tennant" violin by Antonio Stradivari sold at auction for over $2 million.

2 It sure is!

Grammar | **Complete the conversations. Use superlative adjectives.**

1. *A* This airplane is so big.

   B Yeah. It's _____the biggest_____ airplane I've ever been on.

2. *A* It's very easy to get to the airport by subway.

   B Yes. The subway is _____ way to get there.

3. *A* This restaurant isn't really expensive at all.

   B I know. It's _____ restaurant in the city.

4. *A* This subway is very crowded.

   B It sure is. It's always _____ subway line.

5. *A* That's a large cruise ship!

   B It's the *Queen Mary 2*. It's _____ cruise ship in the world.

6. *A* That guy over there is very thin.

   B You're right. He's _____ person I've ever seen.

7. *A* This is a pretty good price for these pants.

   B Yes, it is. Actually, I think this store has _____ prices in the mall.

8. *A* This is a nice gallery, but the new exhibition has some really bad paintings.

   B Yeah. They're some of _____ paintings I've ever seen.

3 About you

Grammar | **Complete the questions with superlatives. Then write true answers.**

1. Where's _the cheapest_ (cheap) place to go shopping around here?

   The cheapest place to go shopping is downtown.

2. And where's _____ (bad) place to go shopping?

   _____

3. Which neighborhood has _____ (nice) restaurants?

   _____

4. What's _____ (quiet) neighborhood in your city?

   _____

5. What's _____ (amazing) building you've ever seen?

   _____

6. What's _____ (busy) street in your city?

   _____

7. What's _____ (wonderful) city you've ever visited?

   _____

8. Where can you buy _____ (delicious) pastries in your city?

   _____

1 Wonders of the earth

Vocabulary **A** Look at the pictures, and complete the puzzle. Then write the answer to the question below.

1. v o l c a n o
2. ___ [ ] ___ ___ ___ ___
3. ___ [ ] ___ ___ ___ ___ ___
4. ___ ___ [ ] ___ ___ ___ ___ ___
5. ___ ___ ___ [ ] ___ ___
6. ___ ___ [ ] ___ ___

What is the most powerful force on the planet? Mother N ___ ___ ___ ___ ___ .

B Complete these sentences with the words from part A.

1. The Grand __Canyon__ in Arizona is 1,600 meters (5,249 feet) deep in some parts.
2. The Pacific _____ is about 10 times larger than the Arctic.
3. K2, the second highest _____ in the world, is 8,610 meters (28,250 feet) high.
4. In the Sahara _____ , temperatures can reach 54 degrees Celsius
   (130 degrees Fahrenheit).
5. Angel Falls in Venezuela is the highest _____ in the world.
6. Mt. Pinatubo in the Philippines is an active _____ . It last erupted in 1991.

2 How wide?

Grammar | Look at the pictures. Complete each question with *How* + adjective. Then write the answers.

1. Q <u>How wide</u> are the Khone Falls on the Mekong River?
   A <u>They're 10.8 kilometers wide.</u>

2. Q _____ is the Amazon Rain Forest?
   A _____

3. Q _____ can it get in Antarctica?
   A _____

4. Q _____ is the Mississippi River?
   A _____

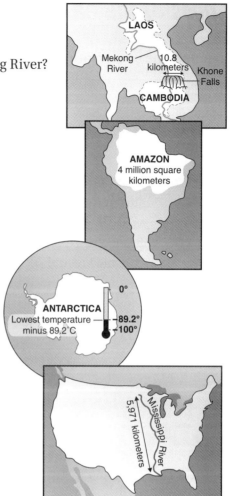

3 Discover New Zealand!

Grammar | Write *How* questions based on the guidebook page. Then answer the questions.

1. Q <u>How long is the Waikato River?</u>
   A <u>It's 425 kilometers long.</u>
2. Q _____
   A _____
3. Q _____
   A _____
4. Q _____
   A _____
5. Q _____
   A _____
6. Q _____
   A _____
7. Q _____
   A _____

Discover New Zealand!

See New Zealand's longest river: the Waikato River – 425 kilometers long

North Island 115,777 square kilometers

Climb New Zealand's highest mountain: Mount Cook – 3,754 meters high

Explore New Zealand's highest waterfall: Arthur R. Sutherland Waterfall – 580 meters high

Visit New Zealand's deepest lake: Lake Hauroko – 462 meters deep

South Island 151,215 square kilometers

450 kilometers

1 Really?

Conversation strategies **Complete the conversations with the sentences in the box.**

It really was.	✓Yeah, it really is.	It sure is.	We really should.
It sure does.	Really? I didn't know that.	They really are.	

1. *Danielle* I think Hawai'i is one of the most interesting states in the U.S.

   Mark <u>Yeah, it really is.</u> Did you know more than one third of the world's pineapples are from Hawai'i?

   Danielle No, I didn't! I know it has eight major islands, though – all from volcanoes.

   Mark Yeah, and it has some of the best surfing beaches.

   Danielle _____ They get the highest waves there.

2. *Maria* Mount Sorak in South Korea is so beautiful, especially in the fall.

   Pete You're right. _____ Have you ever hiked there?

   Maria Uh-huh, I've hiked there several times with my friends.

   Pete _____

   Maria Yeah. I especially love the waterfalls. They're the best.

   Pete I know. _____

3. *Chika* The weather was terrible last weekend.

   Kacie _____ I wanted to go to the beach, but it was too cold.

   Chika So what did you do?

   Kacie Well, I stayed home and watched DVDs.

   Chika That doesn't sound like much fun. I hear next weekend's going to be warm and sunny. We should go to the beach then.

   Kacie _____ . Let's plan on it!

2 *The best and the worst!*

Conversation strategies

Complete the conversations with superlative adjectives for emphasis.

1. *A* Chichén Itzá in Mexico has ____the coolest____ (cool) Mayan ruins. Have you ever been there?

   B Yeah, I had _____ (good) time climbing the pyramids.

2. *A* The food at that restaurant was _____ (bad)!

   B I know, but at least the waiter was nice.

3. *A* How was your weekend?

   B Wonderful! We went to _____ (incredible) lake and rented a boat. We just sailed around for hours!

4. *A* Have you ever hiked the Appalachian Trail?

   B No, unfortunately, I haven't. But I hear it has _____ (amazing) scenery.

3 *It really is the best!*

Conversation strategies

You're camping with your friend. Write responses with *really* or *sure* to show you are a supportive listener. Then add a sentence using a superlative adjective for emphasis.

1. It sure feels good to be on vacation. | It sure does! And camping was the coolest idea!

2. Our hike yesterday was great. | _____

3. We should go swimming in the lake today. | _____

4. It's so nice to be in the country. | _____

4 *About you*

Conversation strategies

Write true sentences about your last vacation or special day. Use superlative adjectives for emphasis.

1. I went __to Costa Rica, and I think their beaches have the softest sand__ .
2. I stayed _____ .
3. I saw _____ .
4. I met _____ .
5. I ate _____ .
6. I visited _____ .

Is that a fact?

1 The coldest continent

Reading   **A** Look at the topics below. Then read the article, and write the number of the paragraph where the topic is explained in detail.

_3_	the driest weather	___ the strongest winds
___	the most time zones	___ the most ice
___	the smallest population	___ the most daylight
___	the farthest south	___ the coldest temperature

AMAZING ANTARCTICA

1 Antarctica is the coldest, windiest, and driest continent on Earth. It's the fifth largest of the world's seven continents. A layer of ice almost 5 kilometers (3 miles) thick covers the island in some places. In fact, 90% of the world's ice is in Antarctica.

2 The weather in Antarctica is the coldest on Earth. The lowest temperature ever recorded, -89.2 degrees Celsius (-128.6 degrees Fahrenheit), was in 1983 at the Vostok Station, an old Russian research base. At the South Pole, the temperature varies from -35 degrees Celsius (-31 degrees Fahrenheit) in the midsummer to -70 degrees Celsius (-94 degrees Fahrenheit) in the midwinter.

3 Antarctica is not only the world's coldest continent but also the driest place on Earth. Sometimes called the world's largest desert, it gets about the same amount of rain each year as the Sahara Desert. Antarctic winds are the strongest on the planet, reaching up to 320 kilometers (199 miles) per hour.

4 Located at the South Pole, Antarctica is the farthest south of any continent. The South Pole gets six months of nonstop daylight from September through March. Then it gets six months of nonstop darkness. And because it's so far south, Antarctica covers the most time zones – all of them!

Vostok Station

5 Explorers first visited Antarctica in 1821. Then in 1899, a Norwegian explorer set up a research station on Antarctica, and for the first time, people could live there. Now there are about 60 research bases there, set up by many different countries. The population of Antarctica grows from about 1,000 in the winter to about 4,000 during the summer. It has the smallest population of any continent.

B Read the article again. Write *T* (true) or *F* (false) for each sentence. Then correct the false sentences.

1. Antarctica is the world's ~~seventh~~ fifth largest continent. __F__

2. 90% of the world's ice is in Antarctica. ___

3. Antarctica gets more rain than the Sahara Desert. ___

4. Antarctica's six months of nonstop daylight begins in March. ___

5. About 1,000 people live in Antarctica during the summer. ___

2 *The dry facts*

Writing | **A** Read the facts about the Sahara Desert. Combine each pair of sentences to form one sentence.

| ❶ The Sahara Desert is the largest desert in the world. It covers 9.1 million square kilometers of land in North Africa. | ❷ The sand dunes are the highest dunes in the world. They are the biggest tourist attraction in the Sahara. | ❸ The Qattara Depression in Egypt's Sahara is one of the lowest points in Africa. It is 133 meters below sea level. | ❹ The Libyan Sahara is the driest place in the desert. It has the least amount of animal or plant life. |

1. The Sahara Desert, the largest desert in the world, covers 9.1 million square kilometers of land in North Africa.

2. _____

_____

3. _____

_____

4. _____

_____

B Write four to six pieces of information about your favorite place. Then combine the facts to make sentences.

Unit 3 Progress chart

Mark the boxes below to rate your progress. ☑ = I know how to . . . ? = I need to review how to . . .	To review, go back to these pages in the Student's Book.
Grammar	
☐ use the superlative form of adjectives	22 and 23
☐ use the superlative with nouns	22 and 23
☐ ask and answer questions using *how* + adjective	24 and 25
Vocabulary	
☐ name 5 human wonders	21, 22, and 23
☐ name 5 natural wonders	21, 24, and 25
Conversation strategies	
☐ use short responses with *really* and *sure* to show I'm a supportive listener	26
☐ use superlative adjectives to emphasize my opinions or feelings	27
Writing	
☐ add information about a place or thing in sentences	29

Family gripes

1 Family obligations

Grammar **Complete the conversations with the correct form of the verbs in the box.**

change	do	help	read	use
clean	do	play	stay	✓ watch

1. **Jeff** When I was young, my parents never let me <u>watch</u> TV.
   Paul Really? Why not?
   Jeff They wanted me _____ books and _____ my imagination, not just watch TV.
   Paul My parents were pretty easygoing about watching TV.
   Jeff What do you mean?
   Paul Well, they just made me _____ my homework first. Then I could watch all the TV I wanted.

2. **Liz** I heard you broke your arm. What happened?
   Kaya My grandmother asked me _____ a lightbulb in the ceiling fan. I lost my balance and fell off a ladder.
   Liz Ouch! What did your doctor say?
   Kaya He told me _____ home for a week.
   Liz Yeah. And you should get someone _____ you next time.

3. **Kyle** I hate Mondays!
   Naomi Me too. They're the worst.
   Kyle Yeah, Monday is when my mom has me _____ the entire house.
   Naomi Really? By yourself? My brother always helps me _____ my chores.
   Kyle Well, my little sister never helps. My mom just lets her _____ video games all day!
   Naomi That's not fair!

2 Gripes and grumbles

Grammar
and
vocabulary

Complete the sentences using the words given.

1. My brother loves anchovies.
   He can't _get me to try one_ .
   (get / try one)

2. My father is pretty strict.
   He always _____ .
   (have / come home early)

3. My parents want me to be a pianist.
   They _____ .
   (make / practice every day)

4. My sister is always watching TV.
   She never _____ .
   (let / have the remote)

5. My daughter is always on her cell phone.
   She always _____ .
   (want / pay the bill)

6. My mom never has enough time to cook.
   She often _____ .
   (ask / prepare dinner)

7. My kids don't like to clean.
   They rarely _____ .
   (help / wash the dishes)

8. My grandfather can't hear very well.
   He always _____ .
   (tell / speak louder)

3 About you

Grammar

Complete these sentences with true information.

1. My parents want me _to go to a really competitive college_ .
2. My best friend often asks me _____ .
3. Our English teacher sometimes has us _____ .
4. I always tell my friend _____ .
5. I can't get my family members _____ .
6. Parents shouldn't let their kids _____ .
7. My friends help me _____ .
8. I can't make my parents _____ .

Family memories

1 My family tree

Vocabulary Look at Kelly's family tree. Then complete the sentences with the words in the box.

✓aunt	brother-in-law	great-grandmother	✓immediate	niece	stepmother
blended	cousin	half brothers	nephew	stepdaughter	uncle

1. My sister, Melissa, is the most talented member of my _____immediate_____ family. She's a great musician.

2. My mother's sister, Jessica, is my _____aunt_____ . I'm Jessica's favorite _____ .

3. Jessica's husband, Max, is my mother's _____ and my _____ .

4. Max and Jessica's son, Evan, is my _____ .

5. Evan is my mother's only _____ .

6. My parents got divorced when I was 12. My father later married Helena. She's my _____ .

7. My father and his second wife had twin boys, Keith and Noah. They're my _____ .

8. With Helena, Keith, and Noah, I grew up in a _____ family.

9. Helena has a daughter from her first marriage. Her name is Kristen. She's my father's _____ .

10. My _____ , Irene, is the oldest member of my extended family. She's my grandmother's mother.

2 *When I was a kid, . . .*

**Complete the conversation with *used to* or *would* and the
verbs given. Sometimes more than one answer is possible.**

Tia Hi, Mom. What are you looking at?

Mom I'm looking at some old pictures from when I was a kid.

Tia Cool. Who's this boy?

Mom That's my friend Jay. He __used to live__ next door to me.
(live)

　We __would spend__ every day together in the summer.
(spend)

Tia Really? Doing what?

Mom We _____ to ride bikes.
(love)

　We _____ our lunches and spend the
(bring)

　whole day riding in the woods.

Tia Cool. What else?

Mom Well, we _____ fishing, and my mom _____ whatever
(go)　　　　　　　　　　　　　　(always cook)

　fish we caught.

Tia It sounds like you had a lot of fun.

Mom We did. We _____ an old black-and-white TV, and we _____
(have)　　　　　　　　　　　　　　　　　　　　　(watch)

　horror movies all the time.

Tia Black-and-white TV? You mean you didn't have a color TV?

Mom No, we didn't. And we didn't have remotes, either.

Tia Wow. I can't even imagine!

3 *About you*

**Are these sentences true or false for you? Write *T* (true) or *F* (false). Then correct
the false sentences.**

1. _F_　When I was a kid, I used to go to the movies on Saturdays.

　　__I didn't use to go to the movies on Saturdays. I would play with my brother.__

2. ___　Our neighbors used to have a pet rabbit.

　　_____

3. ___　I used to hate pizza.

　　_____

4. ___　My parents used to make me go to bed before 9:00.

　　_____

5. ___　I used to ride my bike to school every day.

　　_____

6. ___　My family used to live in a small house in the country.

　　_____

If you ask me, . . .

1 What's your opinion?

Conversation strategies **Read the news items. Then write your opinions using the expressions in the box.**

I don't think	I think	It seems to me (that)
If you ask me,	It seems like	

The percentage of obese children and adolescents has doubled in the last 20 years.

1. _If you ask me, children and adolescents don't exercise enough these days._

90% of British teens learn no foreign languages after the age of 16.

2. _____

Surveys show South Korean teens get a new cell phone every 16 months.

3. _____

Most Japanese high schools don't allow their students to hold part-time jobs.

4. _____

The United States has the world's highest divorce rate.

5. _____

Canadians are now sending 3.4 million text messages per day, or a total of 95.5 million every month.

6. _____

2 I agree.

Follow the instructions and complete the conversations. Use the expressions in the box.

Absolutely.	✓ I agree with you.	That's true.
Definitely.	Oh, I know.	You're right.

1. *Bruno* I think there's a lot of pressure on young couples these days.

   You <u>I agree with you.</u>
   (Tell Bruno you agree.)

   Bruno They work longer hours and still don't make much money.

   You _____
   (Tell Bruno you're in definite agreement.)

2. *Salma* If you ask me, our teachers give us too much homework.

   You _____ I never have any time to spend with my family.
   (Tell Salma you're in absolute agreement.)

   Salma And we never get a break. We even get homework over school vacations.

   You _____
   (Tell Salma she's right.)

3. *Ciara* It seems like a lot of elderly people live alone.

   You _____
   (Tell Ciara her information is true.)

   Ciara It's terrible when families don't invite elderly relatives to live with them.

   You _____
   (Tell Ciara you know.)

3 Don't you agree?

Your friend is telling you his or her opinion. Agree and give an appropriate response.

1. I think kids need cell phones these days.   <u>Definitely. I think they're good in an emergency.</u>

2. If you ask me, movie tickets cost too much.   _____

3. It seems to me that people eat too much fast food.   _____

4. I think everyone should learn a second language.   _____

5. I don't think people take enough vacation time.   _____

Childhood memories

1 Gripes from a househusband

Reading **A Read the blog. What kind of blog is it?**

☐ academic   ☐ news   ☐ personal   ☐ travel

Mario's Blog

Posted by Mario at 3:57 p.m.

....

I'm exhausted! My kids are so lazy. I can't get Joanna, Nancy, and Michael to
help me around the house, no matter how much I nag them. Their clothes,
shoes, and schoolbooks are all over the place. Tonight, their cousins are
coming for dinner. My brother and sister-in-law are bringing their five kids
over here so they can go out for their anniversary. Can you imagine? Eight
kids in the house! In addition, my aunt wants to come over so she can see
all her great-nieces and great-nephews. And she always asks me to make
her favorite dessert – Mardi Gras cake – that takes at least two hours to
prepare. To top it all off, tonight is my wife's tennis club party, so I have to
do all the cooking and cleaning by myself.

It seems to me that my wife could stay home and help out – just this once. She's always going to some
activity. Sometimes it's a co-worker's birthday, sometimes it's her book club, and other times it's her
gym class. I guess I don't mind, because I'm a homebody, but she used to help cook and clean more.
She would do the grocery shopping, and then she'd get the kids to pitch in and clean up while she
started dinner for us.

Lately, she's been too busy. And tonight, the living room is a mess, and dirty dishes are piled up in the
sink. If you ask me, it's too much for one person to do. I know, . . . I'll call my stepbrother and have him
help. I'll ask my mother to make the cake at her house while I go grocery shopping. And maybe my aunt
will help with the cooking. After all, it's all in the family, right?

B Look at the words and expressions. Find them in the blog, and choose the correct meaning.

1. nag _b_   a. talk loudly   b. ask repeatedly   c. laugh quietly
2. great-niece ____   a. your favorite niece   b. your niece's mother   c. your niece's daughter
3. to top it all off ____   a. the final and worst problem is   b. fortunately   c. one good thing is
4. homebody ____   a. someone who doesn't like to go out   b. a housekeeper   c. a personal chef
5. pitch in ____   a. go and play   b. cook   c. help out

C Read the blog again. Then answer the questions.

1. How many children does Mario have? _He has three children._

2. How many of Mario's nieces and nephews are coming for dinner? _____

3. Who used to do the grocery shopping? _____

4. Why is Mario upset with his wife this time? _____

5. What is Mario going to do to get ready? _____

2 Lessons learned

Writing **A** Read the journal entry. Then complete the sentences with the expressions in the box.

In those days	Nowadays	Today	When I was a kid

March 8

I just bought some lemonade from some kids on the corner near my apartment. It brought back so many memories! _____ , I used to make lemonade with my brother. We'd set up a stand in front of our house and sell the lemonade to people walking down the street. _____ , we didn't worry about money, and we drank more lemonade than we sold. _____ , I still remember the lesson that experience taught me — don't drink your profits! I don't think we ever made any money, but it sure was a lot of fun. _____ we have air conditioning, but I still like a cold cup of lemonade on a hot day.

B Write a journal entry about a childhood memory you remember clearly. Use the expressions from part A.

_____
_____
_____
_____
_____
_____
_____
_____

Unit 4 Progress chart

Mark the boxes below to rate your progress. ☑ = I know how to . . . ？ = I need to review how to . . .	To review, go back to these pages in the Student's Book.
Grammar ☐ use *let*, *make*, *have*, *get*, *want*, *ask*, *tell*, and *help*	34 and 35
☐ use *used to* and *would* to talk about memories	36 and 37
Vocabulary ☐ name at least 15 family members	36
Conversation strategies ☐ give opinions with expressions like *I think* and *It seems to me*	38
☐ use expressions like *absolutely*, *exactly*, and *you're right* to agree	39
Writing ☐ use time markers to write about the past and the present	41

1 A bag and a can

Vocabulary Look at the pictures. Complete the sentences with the expressions in the box. Some expressions are used more than once.

a bag of	a box of	a carton of	a package of
a bottle of	a can of	a jar of	

1. In the United States, you can buy
   a bottle of milk or _____ milk.

2. In Thailand, you can buy _____
   curry paste or _____ curry paste.

3. In Japan, you can buy _____
   crackers or _____ crackers.

4. In Australia, you can buy _____
   asparagus or _____ asparagus.

5. In Colombia, you can buy _____
   coffee or _____ coffee.

6. In France, you can buy _____
   soup or _____ soup.

2 *What did Selena buy?*

Vocabulary | Look at the picture. Write what Selena bought at the grocery store.

1. a jar of olives
2. _____
3. _____
4. _____
5. _____
6. _____
7. _____
8. _____

3 *A lot or a little?*

Grammar | Carl is doing his weekly grocery shopping. Circle the best quantifier to complete each of his thoughts.

Hmm . . . we only have **a few** / (**a little**) cheese left in the refrigerator. I guess I'll get some more. And there's **not many** / **not much** butter left, either, so I'll get some of that, too. I don't think that there are **many** / **much** oranges left in the fruit bowl, and I know my roommate likes bananas, so I'll get both. He's such a picky eater. He eats **very few** / **very little** vegetables, but I should get **a few** / **a little** cucumbers, at least. Um . . . the ice-cream section . . . I really want to eat **fewer** / **less** ice cream, but maybe I can buy a light, fat-free kind with **fewer** / **less** calories in it. Well, I think that's all I need. . . .

4 *About you*

Grammar and vocabulary | Complete each sentence with true information. Use a quantifier from the box and a food word. The quantifiers may be used more than once.

a few	fewer	very few
a little	less	very little

1. There are _very few apples_ in my refrigerator.
2. I try to eat _____ every day.
3. I had _____ yesterday.
4. I'm eating _____ these days.
5. There's _____ in my cupboard.
6. I eat _____ than I used to.

1 Prepared foods

Vocabulary | There are ten ways to serve foods in the puzzle. Find the other nine.
Look in these directions (→↓).

B	A	K	E	D	X	L	Y	Q	B
A	B	L	M	A	R	R	T	E	G
R	O	A	S	T	P	A	I	P	R
B	I	C	M	R	Z	W	Y	I	I
E	L	S	M	O	K	E	D	C	L
C	E	D	C	J	E	L	M	K	L
U	D	F	R	I	E	D	P	L	E
E	Z	T	S	T	E	A	M	E	D
D	M	U	X	P	Y	R	I	D	P

2 Smoked bread?

Vocabulary | Cross out the food that is the least likely to go with the preparation.
Then replace it with an appropriate food.

1. smoked ⌐ cheese
   │ turkey
   └ ~~bread~~ fish

2. raw ⌐ fish
   │ ice cream
   └ vegetables

3. boiled ⌐ grapes
   │ eggs
   └ potatoes

4. steamed ⌐ rice
   │ milk
   └ pizza

5. fried ⌐ noodles
   │ yogurt
   └ chicken

6. barbecued ⌐ noodles
   │ beef
   └ lamb

7. pickled ⌐ cabbage
   │ onions
   └ cheese

3 *Too much rice*

Grammar What's the problem? Complete the sentences with *too, too much,*
too many, or *enough.*

1. Martha got __too much__ rice and not __enough__ meat.

2. Sheila ate _____ cupcakes!
   She often eats _____ dessert.

3. This coffee costs _____ !
   It's _____ expensive.

4. Taro drank the sour lemonade
   _____ fast.

5. The soup's not hot _____ .
   And there's _____ salt in it.

6. Alice didn't take the turkey out early
   _____ . Now she won't have
   _____ food for dinner.

4 *About you*

Complete the questions with *too, too much, too many,* or *enough.*
Then write true answers.

1. Do you eat a lot of snacks – do you eat __too many__ ? __I eat three snacks a day.__
2. Do you eat _____ vegetables every day? _____
3. Do you ever feel _____ full after eating a meal? _____
4. Do you exercise _____ – at least twice a week? _____
5. Do you eat _____ for lunch so you don't need a snack later? _____
6. Do you ever eat meals _____ quickly and feel sick? _____
7. Do you drink _____ water – at least 2 liters? _____
8. Do you think you eat _____ fried foods? _____

Whatever you're having.

1 Either way is fine.

Complete the conversation with the expressions in the box.

either one is fine   whatever you're having
either way is fine   ✓whichever is easier for you

Brent   I'm going to cook dinner tonight,
so what would you like? Chicken or steak?

Imani   Well, you're the cook,
so <u>whichever is easier for you</u> .

Brent   No, I want you to choose. I got to decide last
night's dinner menu.

Imani   Well, you know, I really like both,
so _____ .

Brent   OK. I'll cook the chicken. How do you want it tonight? Fried or grilled?

Imani   Oh, _____ . I'm sure whatever you cook will
be delicious.

Brent   OK, I'll grill it. Now, what do you want to drink?

Imani   Oh, _____ . You know me, anything is fine.

Brent   Well, you're certainly easy to please!

Imani   I try.

2 Whatever you want.

**Imagine you are at a friend's house. Respond to each question appropriately to let
your friend decide.**

Friend   Do you want to eat out or get takeout later tonight?

You   <u>Oh, I don't care. Whatever you prefer.</u>

Friend   OK, let's go out. Do you prefer Mexican or Indian food?

You   _____

Friend   Well, I know this great Mexican restaurant. I'll make reservations. 7:00 or 8:00?

You   _____

Friend   Oh, let's make it 7:30. Now, should we drive or take the subway?

You   _____

Friend   Well, driving is easier, so should we take your car or mine?

You   _____

Friend   All right. I'll drive. Now, would you like something to drink? Tea? Coffee?

You   _____

3 I'm OK for now.

Use polite refusal expressions to complete the conversation.

Peggy Would you like some more iced tea?

Nora <u>No, thanks. Maybe later.</u> I've got enough here.

Peggy Gosh, there were a lot of fries here. I still have some left. Would you like a few?

Nora _____ I'm trying to cut down on things like fries. You didn't have much salad. Take some of my carrots.

Peggy _____ You know, they have the best chocolate cake here. You should try some.

Nora _____ I'm trying to eat less sugar, too.

Peggy Oh. Well, are you going to have coffee?

Nora _____

4 Let's have some . . .

Respond to each question by politely refusing or letting the other person decide.

1. Let's have some ice cream. Would you like vanilla or strawberry?

   <u>Either one is fine. Whatever you're having.</u>

2. I'm getting hungry. Do you want something to eat?

   _____

3. There's cake and cookies for dessert. Which would you like?

   _____

4. I'm going to bake a pie. Do you prefer apple or peach?

   _____

5. I'm taking you to lunch today – my treat! Would you like Italian or Thai?

   _____

1 Food alternatives

Reading | **A** Read the article. Circle the helpful foods and products that are mentioned.

DOUBLE DUTY

Did you know that you have a personal beauty spa right in your refrigerator? And did you know that for easy fix-it projects around your home, you simply need to look at your grocery list for help? Here are some ways to make your groceries do double duty.

Hair and face care

Brighter eyes Were you up all night studying for a test, and now it's morning, and your eyes are tired and puffy? Take a few slices of a cold cucumber, and place them over your eyes. Leave them on for about 5 to 10 minutes. Good-bye puffiness, good morning bright eyes!

Clearer skin Uh-oh. You've got a date this weekend, and you just woke up with a pimple! Take a little toothpaste – not too much – and put it on the pimple. Leave it on for at least 5 minutes. Repeat daily if necessary. By Saturday night, your date won't notice a thing!

Lighter hair Do you want some summer highlights and can't afford a hair salon? The next time you're going out in the sun, squeeze some fresh lemon juice into a bowl, and comb it through your hair.

Fix-it projects

Water stains Did you leave a cold glass of water on a wooden table overnight, and now there's a ring on it? You can't make it disappear, but you can lighten it considerably – with toothpaste. Mix equal parts toothpaste and baking soda, and then rub the mixture into the wood with a damp cloth. Wipe it off with a dry cloth.

Clogged drain Is your shower drain clogged, and now the water's taking a long time to go down? Mix equal parts salt, baking soda, and cream of tartar, and then pour it down the drain. Follow with boiling water. Leave it overnight.

Pest remedy

Insect bites One thing about summer you can't control is the bugs. But you can stop them from biting you. White vinegar will deter some pests. Pour some vinegar onto a cloth, and wipe over your skin. The smell goes away after the vinegar has dried, but the bugs won't like the taste of the vinegar. Reapply often.

B Read the article again. Then match the two parts of each sentence.

1. For puffy eyes, _d_
2. To get rid of pimples, ___
3. To lighten your hair, ___
4. To treat a water stain on wood, ___
5. To unclog a drain, ___
6. To deter biting pests, ___

a. wipe vinegar on your skin.
b. put baking soda, cream of tartar, and salt in it.
c. rub toothpaste and baking soda on it.
d. place cucumber slices on them.
e. comb lemon juice through it.
f. put a little toothpaste on them.

40

2 Ethnic eateries

Writing | **A** Read the brochure for a food tour of New York. Add *for example, like,* and *such as* to introduce examples. Sometimes more than one answer is possible.

Food Adventures

There are so many international restaurants in New York, you'll never get bored with the same old food. There are many ethnic eateries in Manhattan, particularly downtown below 34th Street. _____ , if you like Middle Eastern food, you can get *falafel* at Rainbow Falafel, just off Union Square. If you're craving Korean food,

_____ *bulgogi* (beef barbecue), head to Koreatown, between 32nd and 34th Streets. If you're dying for treats from Argentina, _____ *empanadas*, Gauchas on First Avenue is for you. Get the idea? So, if you need something different, or something from another culture, downtown Manhattan is a food-lover's dream.

B Write a brochure or an article about special foods, crafts, or souvenirs in your city or country. Give examples of what you can eat or buy using *for example, like,* and *such as.*

_____
_____
_____
_____
_____
_____
_____

Unit 5 Progress chart

Mark the boxes below to rate your progress. ✓ = I know how to . . . ? = I need to review how to . . .	To review, go back to these pages in the Student's Book.
Grammar ☐ use quantifiers like *a little, a few, very little, very few,* etc.	44 and 45
☐ use *too, too much, too many,* and *enough*	47
Vocabulary ☐ talk about food using expressions like *a jar of, a can of, a box of,* etc.	43 and 44
☐ name at least 8 different ways of serving food	46
Conversation strategies ☐ respond to questions by letting another person decide	48
☐ use expressions like *No, thanks. I'm fine* to refuse an offer politely	49
Writing ☐ use *for example, like,* and *such as* to introduce examples	51

Unit 6 Managing life

Making plans

1 What are you doing after work?

Grammar   Circle the best verb forms to complete the conversations.

1. *Ahmed*   Hey, Finn. What **do you do** / **are you doing** after work tonight?

    Finn   I have no plans. **I just go** / **I'm just going** home. Why? What are you up to?

   Ahmed   Well, **I go** / **I'm going** to the gym around 5:00, but after that, I have no plans.

    Finn   OK. Well, maybe **I'm stopping by** / **I'll stop by** later.

   Ahmed   Sure. **I rent** / **I'll rent** a movie.

    Finn   Oh, no. I just remembered. **I have** / **I'm having** a doctor's appointment at 6:00.

   Ahmed   That's OK. **I'm waiting** / **I'll wait** for you to watch the movie. Just come right over when you're done.

    Finn   All right. **I'm going to be** / **I'll be** there by 7:30.

   Ahmed   Don't be late!

2. *Leah*   Hi, Mom. I was just calling to let you know that **I take** / **I'm going to take** a 5:30 train this Friday.

    Mom   Great, honey. **I'm meeting** / **I'll meet** you at the station.

    Leah   No, that's OK. **I won't need** / **I'm not needing** you to pick me up. **I'm getting** / **I'll get** a taxi.

    Mom   OK. **Do you bring** / **Are you bringing** your friend?

    Leah   Yeah. Janice **will come** / **is coming** with me.

    Mom   Oh, how nice. I can't wait to meet her!

    Leah   I'm sure **you're going to like** / **you like** her. See you Friday!

2 *Let me check my schedule.*

Grammar   Look at Millie's weekly planner, and complete the conversation.

Monday	**Thursday**
~~art exhibit with Jenna~~	6:30 guitar lesson, as usual
Tuesday	**Friday**
6:30 guitar lesson	plans with Heidi?
Wednesday	**Saturday** dinner with Greg
5:45 eye doctor appointment	**Sunday** 7:00 flight

Raquel   Let's have dinner together this week.

Millie   Sounds good. I'd love to catch up with you.

Raquel   How about Saturday?

Millie   Hmm . . . I can't Saturday. I 'm meeting / 'm going to meet Greg for dinner (meet).

Raquel   Well, then, what about Thursday?

Millie   That won't work, either. I _____ (have).

Raquel   Oh, yeah, I forgot. Well, I'm free next Sunday.

Millie   Sunday, I'm leaving for Dallas. My flight _____ (leave).

Raquel   And Friday?

Millie   I have tentative plans with Heidi.

Raquel   Oh? What are you guys doing?

Millie   I don't know. I _____ (call) on Friday to see what's up.

Raquel   OK. Well, then why don't *you* pick a day?

Millie   Let's see . . . Oh, Wednesday, I _____ (have). Actually, you know what? Jenna canceled our plans to see an art exhibit tonight. Do you want to go?

Raquel   Sure. I _____ (go) with you!

3 *About you*

Grammar   Answer the questions with true information.

1. What are you going to do tonight?

   _____

2. Are you doing anything special this weekend?

   _____

3. Do you have any appointments this month? If yes, who with?

   _____

4. Who are you having dinner with tomorrow night?

   _____

5. What do you think you'll do when you finish this exercise?

   _____

1 Make up your mind.

Vocabulary **A** Complete the *make* and *do* expressions. Use the definitions to help you.

1. make a ___living___ = work to earn money
2. make a good _____ = make someone think of you positively
3. make a _____ = make a positive change
4. do your _____ = try your hardest
5. make up your _____ = decide
6. make _____ of = make jokes about and laugh at
7. make _____ = make certain
8. make a _____ = get something wrong
9. do the _____ = figure out the numbers
10. make _____ = seem logical

B Complete the conversations with the *make* and *do* expressions from part A.

1. *A* Which computer are you going to get?
   Did you ___make up your mind___ ?
   B No. I can't decide. I like this one, but it's expensive.
   A Well, buy the best you can afford.
   It doesn't _____ to buy a cheap one.
   B Yeah, you're right. I need to _____
   and look at all the numbers before I decide.

2. *A* Are you all prepared for your interview? You look
   great. I'm sure you'll _____ .
   B Thanks. I really want this job with the children's
   charity. I've always wanted to _____
   in people's lives. I know it's not well paid, but it's how
   I want to _____ .
   A Well, good luck. You'd better leave now
   to _____ you get there on time.

3. *A* I have to give a presentation to the class today.
   I'm so afraid I'll _____ and say
   something wrong.
   B Well, just _____ , and I'm sure
   everything will be fine.
   A I know. I'm just scared that the other students
   will _____ me.

2 *Let's ask Daphne.*

 Grammar   Circle the best expression to complete each sentence.

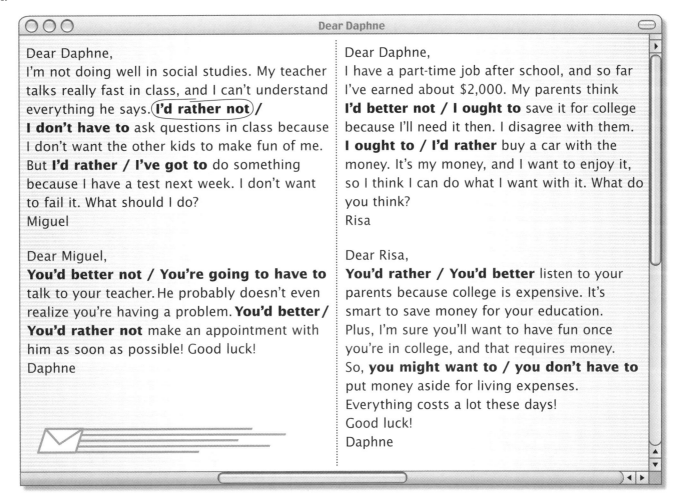

Dear Daphne,
I'm not doing well in social studies. My teacher talks really fast in class, and I can't understand everything he says. (**I'd rather not**) /
I don't have to ask questions in class because I don't want the other kids to make fun of me. But **I'd rather / I've got to** do something because I have a test next week. I don't want to fail it. What should I do?
Miguel

Dear Miguel,
You'd better not / You're going to have to talk to your teacher. He probably doesn't even realize you're having a problem. **You'd better / You'd rather not** make an appointment with him as soon as possible! Good luck!
Daphne

Dear Daphne,
I have a part-time job after school, and so far I've earned about $2,000. My parents think **I'd better not / I ought to** save it for college because I'll need it then. I disagree with them. **I ought to / I'd rather** buy a car with the money. It's my money, and I want to enjoy it, so I think I can do what I want with it. What do you think?
Risa

Dear Risa,
You'd rather / You'd better listen to your parents because college is expensive. It's smart to save money for your education. Plus, I'm sure you'll want to have fun once you're in college, and that requires money. So, **you might want to / you don't have to** put money aside for living expenses. Everything costs a lot these days! Good luck!
Daphne

3 *About you*

 Grammar   Write true sentences about these topics.

1. something you've got to do this week
   I've got to make up my mind about a summer job.

2. something you'd better do before next week

3. two things you don't have to do this week

4. something you feel you ought to do this year

5. something you'd rather do now instead of homework

6. three things you're going to have to do tomorrow

1 I can't talk right now.

Conversation strategies Ming-li and Ivana want to make plans, but they always call each other at the wrong time. Complete the expressions they use to end their conversations.

1
Hey, Ming-li. It's Ivana.

Hi, Ivana. Listen, I can't talk. I have to walk the dog. I've got _to go_ .

2
Hey, Ivana. I'm back. What's up?

Oh, no. Now I can't talk. I'm going to my yoga class. I've got _____ .

3
Oh, great, you're home. Have a minute?

Ivana, my mom's calling me on my cell phone. I'll _____ .

4
Me again. I can finally talk.

Hey. Listen, I just sat down to dinner with a friend. I'd _____ .

5
Hey. I just got back from dinner.

Ivana, it's midnight! Can I _____ tomorrow morning?

6
So, I got tickets to Friday's concert. Do you want to go?

Sure! Listen, call me Friday. I'm going _____ . I have a meeting.

2 Talk to you later!

Circle the best response. Then write the shorter form.

1. *A* Oh, hi. Can I call you back later?
   B _Sure. Talk to you later._
   a. Sure. I'd better go.
   b.) Sure. I'll talk to you later.

2. *A* I'm really sorry. I've got to go out in two minutes.
   B _____
   a. No problem. I've got to go, too. Bye.
   b. No problem. I'm not busy.

3. *A* Let's talk tomorrow.
   B _____
   a. OK. Now's a good time.
   b. OK. I'll catch you later.

4. *A* Well, anyway, I'd better go.
   B _____
   a. OK. I'll see you later.
   b. OK. I can't talk right now.

5. *A* I'm so glad you called. It was fun to catch up.
   B _____
   a. Yeah, I'll call you later.
   b. Yeah, it was nice talking to you, too!

6. *A* I'd better go. I'm late.
   B _____
   a. That's OK. I'm free now.
   b. That's OK. I'd better go, too.

3 The end?

Imagine you're trying to leave your house to go to your English class, but four friends call you. Try to end each conversation. Then use a "friendly" good-bye.

1. *Liliana* Hi, it's me. Listen, I have a problem. Do you have some time to talk?
   You _Not really. I've got to go to English class. Can I call you back?_
   Liliana OK.
   You _Talk to you later._

2. *Hans* Hi, it's Hans. Are you busy right now? I need to ask you a question.
   You _____
   Hans No problem.
   You _____

3. *Doug* Hey! Guess what? I have some exciting news for you!
   You _____
   Doug Fine. Call me when you get home later.
   You _____

4. *Louisa* Hi! It's Louisa. I didn't understand the homework. Did you?
   You _____
   Louisa All right. Well, maybe we can meet in the library tomorrow.
   You _____

1 Getting organized

A Read the article. Then add the correct heading to each section.

Save money	Save space	Save time

Tips that $AVE

Whether your schedule is crazy, your apartment is cluttered, or your budget is mismanaged, here are some tips to get more organized.

_____

Do you find it difficult to find really good birthday presents because you wait until the last minute? And then do you spend hours in the stores because you can't find anything you like?

Whenever you're shopping and you see a gift at a great price, buy it and put it in your closet. When a special occasion comes up and you need a gift for someone, you'll have a selection of things to choose from. You won't have to make a special trip for last-minute shopping.

Do you ever pay bills late because you lose them in all the papers and clutter in your home? Well, if you need a system for paying your bills on time, this should do the trick. When a bill comes in, open it immediately and circle the due date. Put it in a special box on your desk. Keep your checkbook, a couple of pens, envelopes, and plenty of stamps next to the box. When it's time to pay, everything you need is right at your fingertips.

_____

Magazines can take over your home before you know it. If you don't have time to read your magazines

cover to cover, tear out the items you want to save. Divide a notebook into sections, such as "How-To Projects," "Recipes," "Interesting Articles," and "Things to Buy." Put your articles in the notebook. Then recycle the rest of the magazine. Or, make a photocopy of the articles you want, and give the magazine to a friend.

Buy brightly colored baskets or boxes for your shelves to store smaller items neatly. Label them with their contents. Your shelves will look neater, and you'll have more space for your larger items. Hang single shelves above doorways to store things you rarely use. Place low shelves in your closet to take advantage of unused space.

_____

Save for a rainy day, little by little. It's easy to make progress if you give yourself a weekly allowance. Try to spend less than your allowance each week. Put the remaining money in an envelope. At the end of each month, put the money in your bank account.

It's the little habits that count. Have you added up the cost of those cappuccinos you buy every morning? If you spend $3.50 on coffee five days a week, that adds up to $910 a year! By doing without fancy drinks and making your coffee at home, you can save a bundle. You might want to try packing a lunch instead of eating at the local café, too — this habit can also save you hundreds a year.

B Find these words and expressions in the article. Match them with the definitions.

1. do the trick _g_
2. is right at your fingertips ___
3. take advantage of ___
4. a rainy day ___
5. count ___
6. doing without ___
7. a bundle ___

a. make use of
b. a time when you need money
c. not having
d. a lot of money
e. is where you need it
f. make a difference
g. be a solution

C Read the article again. Then write *T* (true), *F* (false), or *D* (doesn't say).

1. ⊤ Buy gifts cheaply when you see them; you can decide who they're for later.
2. ___ You can save money if you pay your bills late.
3. ___ If you don't have time to read your magazines, just recycle them.
4. ___ You can save space on your shelves if you put lots of small things into boxes.
5. ___ It's better to keep your money in an envelope than a bank.
6. ___ You should make more food at home.

2 *Making room*

Writing

A Read the article. Add *as long as*, *provided that*, and *unless* to link ideas. Sometimes more than one answer is possible.

> Your closet is overflowing, and you need to make room for new clothes. How do you decide what to do with all your old clothes? First, get a box and put in everything you hardly ever wear, _____ they aren't clothes for special occasions.
>
> Give them all to a charity store _____ you have some valuable clothes you can sell. Next, use the "two-season rule." Separate your remaining clothes by season. If it's winter, put your winter clothes back in the closet. Buy some under-the-bed boxes for your off-season clothes. If it's summer, store all your sweaters under your bed, _____ the space under your bed isn't already cluttered!

B Write a short article giving advice about how to reduce clutter, save money, or save time. Try to use *as long as*, *provided that*, and *unless* to link ideas.

Unit 6 Progress chart

Mark the boxes below to rate your progress. ✔ = I know how to . . . ? = I need to review how to . . .	To review, go back to these pages in the Student's Book.
Grammar ☐ talk about the future using *will*, *going to*, the present continuous, and the simple present	54 and 55
☐ use *ought to*, *have got to*, *would rather*, *had better*, etc.	56 and 57
Vocabulary ☐ use at least 12 expressions with *do* or *make*	56
Conversation strategies ☐ use at least 5 different expressions to end a phone conversation	58
☐ say good-bye in an informal, friendly way	59
Writing ☐ use *as long as*, *provided that*, and *unless* to link ideas	61

Notes

Notes

Notes

Notes